Poems from a Squeegee Kid

Cheryl Fountain, BSW

To Natasha.
Where ever you are in life you can change your circumstances.
May your life be full of beautiful inspiration xo Cheryl

Poems From a Squeegee Kid

Copyright © 2022 Cheryl Fountain

All rights reserved. No part of this publication may be used or reproduced in any manner whatsoever without written permission of the author, except in the case of brief quotations embodied in critical articles or reviews.

For information contact : www.cherylfountain.com

Cover design by Lorraine Shulba

Published by: Raspberry Press

ISBN: 978-1-7773105-4-7

First Edition: April 2022

Dedication:

To my teen self and the trials and tribulations she faced. And to my friend Pam. I do not know if you made it. You are a beautiful spirit, and I love you dearly.

Table of Contents

INTRODUCTION..i
1..- 3 -
2..- 5 -
3..- 7 -
4..- 9 -
5..- 11 -
INDIVIDUAL..- 13 -
7..- 15 -
8..- 17 -
9..- 19 -
10..- 21 -
11..- 23 -
12..- 25 -
13..- 27 -
14..- 31 -
15..- 35 -
16..- 37 -
17..- 39 -
CONVINCING ANGLES OF ADDICTION..................- 43 -
19..- 47 -
20..- 49 -
LITTLE THINGS...- 51 -
22..- 53 -
23..- 55 -
24..- 59 -

25	- 61 -
NAMELESS LOVE	- 63 -
27	- 65 -
A MEETING FOR LIFE	- 67 -
29	- 69 -
30	- 71 -
WASTE	- 73 -
32	- 75 -
BOREDOM	- 77 -
THE ONE EARED RABBIT	- 79 -
GRAVE	- 81 -
LOVE'S INNOCENCE	- 83 -
PEOPLE	- 89 -
BEGINNING	- 93 -
PROBLEM	- 95 -
DAY TIME DRAMA	- 97 -
HOSTAGE CRISIS	- 99 -
FOR WHOM THE WORDS SPEAK	- 101 -
43	- 103 -
MAGIC LOVE	- 107 -
A FRIENDS LOST IDENTITY	- 109 -
FAILURE	- 111 -
47	- 115 -
AFTERWORD	- 121 -
DEFINITIONS	- 123 -
ABOUT THE AUTHOR	- 126 -

INTRODUCTION

When I was young I experienced homelessness and squeegeed to survive. Squeegeeing is a way for street youth to make an income by washing car windshields with a squeegee (a long handled sponge with a rubber edge often seen at gas stations). Squeegeeing was a popular political topic in the late 1990's in the city of Toronto when I was living on the street. The city was trying to pass a by-law to outlaw squeegeeing because squeegeeing was seen as a nuisance.

There are different ways to make an income while living on the street, and not many are legal. Squeegeeing was quite enterprising and required a strong work ethic, materials, and customer service skills. To start squeegeeing all that was needed was to panhandle enough money to buy a bucket, a squeegee, and liquid dish soap. Next steps were to find a water source, (such as an outdoor tap), fill the bucket with water, add a squirt of dish soap, carry the bucket to a street corner, and wait for the traffic light to turn red. When the light turned red, the persons would carry the wet, soapy, squeegee into stopped traffic, and ask people if they wanted their windshield cleaned. It was important to clean quickly and finish before the light turned green in order to get out of traffic safely.

In the late 1990's newspapers printed articles citing that squeegee kids made more than the Prime Minister of Canada, and were making a dollar a minute. This was grossly over-embellished. A red-light itself might last one minute, and usually drivers gave spare change, and it could be pennies. The kids lived in shelters, in alleys, in trash hotels, with no family support, recovering from or still living with a bundle of traumas. Some faced addiction, mental illness, and post-traumatic stress from family or societal experiences. They had run away from thing such as neglect, physical abuse, emotional abuse, substance abuse in the home, molestation, and other violence. The media framing squeegeeing as a luxury, that people were doing this for fun or to be deviant, infuriated me, and still infuriates me today.

I tried to find employment but I did not have a proper address or phone number for an employer to reach me (this was well before cell phones were commonplace or accessible). Plus, I think the way my clothes looked would have made employers toss my resume as soon as walked away, as my clothes were often very worn and stained. I experienced a lot of darkness during this time. I had friends who I lost to drugs. All of my friends were running away from something. Every single person I met on the street was highly intelligent. The one way I was different from most other street kids was that I attended school, and kept suitable grades. I am still surprised I made it through high school as my attendance was poor. I also did not have support from teachers or school staff. The principal at my school had even pulled me into a session to tell me that people like me do not make it into university. I always made sure to show up and study for tests despite the lack of encouragement and the life challenges I faced. I was accepted into university, and with help from a boyfriend's mom and my brother, I was able to leave the street and start a more comfortable life. It took years to emotionally, mentally, and physically heal from life on the street.

I also had a loving family where I could have returned. There was obviously family issues, as I chose living on the street over being at home. However, I have a sense that my family issues were not as serious as many of my friends who also were living on the street. No one spoke of what happened to them or why they had run away.

These poems are tribute to my teen self, and to my friends. The poems are dark, they are philosophical, they are heavy, and they remind me of the way many teens experience emotions and thoughts. Emotions are enormous for teens and youth, and some adults seem to have forgotten this, or maybe have blocked this truth out as a survival mechanism.

I came across these poems recently. I had sent them printed by a dot-matrix printer to my mom as a gift for her 50th birthday when I was in my first year of university. She later gave the poems back to me. I am grateful she did as I am now able to give my teen self the voice she wanted heard.

Publishing these poems was a dream of my teen self. However, she lacked the confidence and did not have the support to do so. By publishing these, I am honouring my teenage self, and am transmitting through time the support she needed back then.

Despite harsh emotions, there is also a mystical quality in the following poems as I have always been aware of transpersonal psychology, magic, and otherworldly philosophies. There is tough language, anger, love, and some gentleness as well. Some of the poems witness that certain people are valued over others in society, based from the predominate capitalistic culture's premise "you are valuable if you work and contribute to the economy". People look down at other people, treating people poorly when they do not fit within society or fit the ideals of capitalism.

All forty-seven poems are written by my young self, living on the street, trying to make sense of life, love, sometimes journeying into a fantasy land, while at the same time witnessing how people treat each other. I came to a realization, living on the street you are no longer seen as a person, you are treated as an object— a "squeegee kid".

"If you can't be good be careful."
-My dad

1

Against all worlds,
Painful strength disregards,
Insanity, illness, confusion.
For when Time sees
Behind the eye
Truths, immortality, frankness.

Whence come strength,
Power unknown,
Greed.
Senseless peace, mind;
Thoughts ravelling through and toward the light.

Burn candle
melt upon the sun.
Roast the stars
So that they may shine forever.
Keep my stars
in a black box,
hidden from time, and time alone
to express my greed.
Forget the sun, it is too big
For eyes to perceive all at once.

2

The night's shadowed grace
Entwines continuous minds.
Bed bugs savour the taste
Of dusty bed sheets
Only to find
The absence of prey.

A candle is lit
To tease the moon.
A hand softly maneuvers the flame.
Pass through and back again,
A tunnel without an exit;
Trapped?

Continuously pacing
Fearful tears fall
Screams of rage echo
Down the winding hall.
Someone hear!
(no one to call).

Frightfully clawing
at a black sheeted wall,
Tearing bricks to dust
Curling in a ball.

Escaping the pain
Misery
of being alone.
Sunshine breaks through
the dark,
deserted hall.

3

Remember.
Flaunt desirous Flesh
Loose taste,
Nothing,
Nothing to hear
Facing a shattered glass mirror.
Laughing, sobbing,
Nothing.

Peace, mind,
Late traveller,
Scientifically defined.

Suns, moons, stars.
The galaxy henceforth
Unrecognizable plains.
Never mind Nothing,
Nothing is insane.

4

Underestimate extremities.
A bird sings at the crack of dawn
Peaceful song.
Nothing worldwide
Can heal, can speak
Truths.

Mental confliction
Scares the bird away
Flying far
and wide
Seeing the whole view.
Sights above level ground reveal
A knowledge
Fair and Unknown
to the average kind.

Never mind complications,
Accusations, worldwide confusions,
Senseless completion
Of painful rain
soothing the heart.

Broken, falsely,
forcing demands.
Hear me, here?
Forget nonsense,
Release time,
Brainwashed, violent,
Morbid mind.

5

Flowing, taunting,
seeking lust.
Fighting, striking,
falling down.
Forces of magnum
farce the poles of freedom.
Locked out of mind.
Sighting confusions lost time
Naivety destroys
Natures Truths.
Nothing can benefit from
The worship of stale air.

6
INDIVIDUAL

Pictures are not pictures
designed by the norm.
White picket fences,
a safe desert storm.

Thoughts come in mixtures
Perfection is not owned
Out of similar senses,
Nature is cloned.

Easy life is easy play.
The sun breaks through
every day.
Nothing new, nothing old.
The day time ends with
Miles of gold.

7

Although I believe the feeling real
Control is used to blind
My self-protecting mind.

Dear self,
Rise up, Shine!
You need real emotion
To see how love can be.

You have lost yourself in
A twisted lovers net.
Before, scarring your every desire.
Do not let the control hide
What could once again
Develop inside.

Do not deny yourself from peaceful truth
To fly away without knowing
What and where the ground truly is.
You need your whole self,
Drown in tears
Do not let the control
Make you trust your fears.

Please wake up
From the charming control
Use strength, wherever it is,
Use light, stabbing bright light.
Let yourself and truth shine through.
For the only one who can develop true love
The only one is you.

8

I sit here and wonder where to find my strength.
I thought I was under the guard of a convincing state.
Now I realize my lack of control
With it I may lose the trust of my soul.

How far into this begotten net am I tangled?
Where are the scissors to set me free?
Confusion entwines my continuous mind,
Why can't love just be?

The key I held to my heart was stolen
By a powerful, greedy man.
He opens and closes my love at his will
Leaving me struggling to understand.

If it be only but control
How come the thought of him won't flee
My troubled head, My empty bed
What the hell happened
To poor protected me?

In dreams I disguise
My timeless absence.
They speak to me of my reality,
Piecing together change
Making sense.

Crazed understanding of senseless words
Seem to give longing security.
When will the time come
To set myself free
From his trap?

I'll find the light
Someway
Somehow,
Sometime within my eternity.

9
STRUGGLE

When motivation is lost
Nothing is gained
Head hung addicts
Frustrate their dreams

Morning rises
Night falls
Time is of essence
or it just rolls
Along a circular path,
nothing new
nothing old
Except that aching feeling,
churning the addicts soul.

Persisting on thoughts of a new rising sun
Some day
Some way
This thought can be done.

10

Feeding the rat race
Pour it all down,
the grime, the slime, sour lime.
Watch their festering mutation,
Scowl at their pain.
Laugh aloud
To block out their screams.

Hallowed out fire pit
Burning through the ground
Their moss eaten veins
Screech,
with absorptions mound.

False hopes dissipate
through reflectional steam.
Shattered glass pricks slaughtered wrists,
Tears
fountain the salty stream
Forging skins pale domain
Invading cellular storage,
Erasing forgotten memories.
Look deep inside and crush your heart.

11

The clouds I see above are only gases.
Before they were a place of rest.
Where my guardian angel would stand
Watching my every smile,
My every tear that would roll down my innocent cheek.
Now she stands on nothing but gases.

The sun is a blazing mass of plasma.
Before I thought the sun was a god.
He would bring forth a smile on my face
And light up the shadows
Making my playground safe.
Now the sun creates the shadows.

The people around me exist.
Before I was challenged by myself and consciousness.
I would dream up myself with many friends
Made of air.
No one would interfere.
But now they all exist.

12

Twisting and turning
Round and round
Devastating aroma
Feeding through the ground.

Singing and strumming
Up and down
No one to hear
Past the darkening frown.
Sitting and staring
People passing
by and by.
Lost in eternity
Tears form eyes.

Sleeping and dreaming
fears and screams
turning and turning
with knowledge meant to demean.

Children and debts
And cries of pain
Let down the emotion
Within the gentle rain.

Invalid decisions
Waiting for time
to Pound out security
Disease, and Device.

Strangeness screams out
Normality's lies
Difference is everywhere
Behind everyone's eyes.

Oddness and illusion
Fearful tears fall
A kiss to hold on
to a heart
worth so much more.

Without hugging strength
Forced to fall down
And buried
In self-deceit.

13

Bending thoughts crack times immortality.
Sleeping lies change people's morality.
Historical beliefs build futures' goals.
Smashing pulses keep thinkers in their roles.

Awaiting childish lights and charms
How could truth cause so much harm?
Awaken the dead with glowing eyes.
Perched on a sheltered transfusion of lies.

Professional cons
Can do no wrong
Until they are shown
Their cheating lies full blown.

Ha, Ha!
Devastational crap.
Sit back down
or you will get a slap.
On the wrist
On the hand
On any mortal part.

You think you are so strong
But you are completely wrong
WE are all elements of TIME.

Quarreling again?
There is no use
Why not coil your neck in a noose.
It will save you pain,
harm and hunger
It will keep you above
The tide that tows you under
And into the depths of disbelief
Resting on a wasted wretched wreath.
But no.
You can prove me wrong.
For not everyone was born
is born into wrong.
So sing your damn song.
Ignore those below.
"If we stop giving them money
it will stop them so..."
Why not? Sure!
Ignore the beggar, the artist, the NEED.
Without your petty change
They will die from your greed.

Selfish asses
who flaunt the streets with scowls
Rake up the corpses
Hide them under towels.
If the corpses smell
Spray them with perfume
to cover their mess.
If you care speak in peace you rest.

But most would sneer
And walk away
Again isolating the streets
Due to human decay.

If you can't stand me
then die!
I am just the same as you,
I laugh, I cry.
I bellow out in fear
But life has not been as dear to me
As it has been to you.
Not that my life is worse,
I am still so young
I have a lot to do to appear as strong.

So fine,
Continue your hateful speeches.
Your annoyance I laugh at
And learn your deceit.
Your thoughts to me could be valid
So why not talk to me
and see I am not an invalid.
Just relax and see me
As you would see anyone else.

14

The bus ride
Loopy
Twisted and spun
Like a misplaced vine,
Belonging to none.

Laughter, insecurity, blindness
SMACK
Reality
Hidden for so long.

Delusional eyes
Pierce on the child of grace
Nervous energy tingles
Her expressionless face.

Watching the watch
of time, of need
Awaiting the rumble
of transportation's seed.

She never really understood
How lonely it could be
Being alone
Lonelier than perceived.

A companion builds her whole
Joining to halves of the same soul.
Now physically parted
She awaits in fear
Until the time allows
The joining
The wait sincere.

Above the sky seems pale
seems dull
And the clouds
with rain are full.
The wind sings
soft tunes in her mind
The nervous feeling
she struggles to bind.

People pass
she shatters like glass
Broken on the floor
escaping through her door
Through her mind
into rhyme
With swindling thoughts
Breathing in
Breathing out
Relaxation is taught.

She stares at the page
Part way through the book,
Planning futures plot
"Just one look"
The page is blank.

Capabilities are endless
unless self-devised,
Relentlessly provoking failure
with Transfusions of lies.

Let go of expectations
Let the soul fly
In freedom are the answers
The future will lie ahead
Of torment, illness, disease
Quit hiding fingers
Underneath shirt sleeves.
Awake
Cry out in peace
"I love life
And life loves me!"

15

Although your heart corrodes with disease
It is your mind that keeps you at ease.
Forget forgotten memories lost
They only make thinking cost
Millions of senses defined by hell.
Fuck you,
oh dear,
hope everything is well!

There is no use
Teasing the Muse
For logic and math are just an excuse.
We have destroyed magic's soul
We have dragged our world into a hell hole.
Tiny children close their eyes
Unknowing how pointless their little lives.

No matter how bright you shine
To the sky you are dust in its eye.
Goodbye worthy honest hope.
Good bye.

16

Nothing good receives the slice of pie.
Honesty and realism is denied
In this selfless, greedy plain.
Riches consume poor.
Struggling, waisted lives
Eyes withhold arrogant beliefs,
Forgetting compassion
and devouring gold.
Take, take, take,
Nothing to give
Hide smiling faces
Tear dreams apart
Limit happy intending hearts.
Begin peaceful rules.
Steal equality's bounds
Brainwash future leaders,
Teach them how to frown.
See only what lies beyond
Concerning lasting faults
Tiered, destructive crates
of death-defying rates
Burning through the ground
and into the grave.

17
FATAL EXISTENCE

Questions arise beneath the waves
how sheltered beings
think you are wrong.
Truths cause fears
Fears consuming time,
Scared to tears
Mirrors haunt dishevelled sight.

Stare into the nothing;
Black, coated sky.
Create time alone
(Waving goodbye
one last time)
Along the dark long road.

Send the stars
Exploding to dust
Poor injured TIME
as Silence trades the face of nothing,
Creating an existence
facing triads of grace.

Time,
Memory
of Lust
Bow down skyclad
Teasing eternal trust.
Lost
Stolen
Broken.

The eye can see
        beyond the mask
          of charm
           of beauty
          and device.
Safely it laughs at greedy martian sights.

Each day entwined
in mystery
pain
and deceit
Who will be there
to pick up from defeat
when time rolls on?
Yet the eye cannot perceive the truths that lie beyond.

Who can tell
What will go wrong.
Hope
and dreams
help perceive
Out coming lines of plot.
Yet the greed,
the hunger,
the selfish lies
Can erase all that has been taught.

Please
Sit yourself down
Undo your frown
And watch the world spin round.
For quiet and ease
can cure disease
of wasted
Flesh eaten hell.

18
CONVINCING ANGLES OF ADDICTION

There were but five
Children of the night
Tight mortal souls
Enlightened with delight.

Once insanely bound
Innocent eyes
Faded
With ear catching lights
Enhanced sounds surrounding
Remoteless humour.

Sleep; children of five
-prophesied the light
Rest until the coming night
Forget time caressing eternity
Dream
Hope
For your lost identity.

The children never slept
~Fell into a dream
Insomnia blown up their nose
Hoping to reach reality
Driven in insane prose.

"Thank you pain
Absorb it through your veins
Running to your shocking brain"
—chanting heart beats flow
Four escape their fears
Sam fell in tears
Drowned.

His loss excited the dark children's lore
Moped with their fate
"No more shall go!"

Flying? Conceptual truth
But don't flap your arms
You're falling goof.

Pieces of Jack upon the forest floor.

Lacking duel strength
The remaining trio sobbed lightly
"We will stick together
Before the eyes of the almighty."

Baptised into a Christian sphere
Bob jonesed out and bought some weed.
Ideas blossomed in his mind.

A coiled noose,
His neck entwined
Found early Sunday morning
Stretched like a goose.

Three funerals drove
Dying deities down
The two remaining addicts
Burrowed in frown.

"We shall not fly,
Slip, fall, or hang
Let's cut the shit
Cure our diseased brains."

To Dave this change
Strengthened his soul
But Chris snapped
Like a faded photo
Into the realm of the insane.

Dave grew and formed
An impetuous societal state.
Married, employed
Against the devastating
Dreams

Hearing Chris's piercing screams.
Dave's clock is never behind
Nor forward.
He has forgotten
How grand his reward.

His three young children
Grew fond of the bottle
Genetic addictions flourished
Into their blind motto.

"Excuse me sir
Are you doing well?
Smashed metal and leaking gas
Has sent your kids to hell."

The morning dial
Of an empty phone
Dave's slit wrists
And shot wife
Ends the tale
Of horror.

19

The heart
shies
at a man's replies
Nervous energy
driving lusting insanity.

Watching
a daughter
and a man laugh
Knowing, in a short time
will only last
until a heart-filled goodbye.

The heart is crushed
Acknowledging a man's love
Ideal
Always searching
For something perfect
Something real.

But nothing is perfect
and nothing is real
When emotions turn
The cyclic wheel.

The heart sees
Ideals' disease
Remaining
Undertowed in love

Yet the beginning spark
Has faded,
Ideally shaded
and Loyalty is obeyed.

20

What exactly happened?
A loss of faith,
Respect, trust?
Lacking insecurity, I no longer know.

He doesn't listen
He never listens
Why can't he just listen once?
Stupidly I jumped out of his grasp.
I never wanted to be in it though.

He never used to want me
How come when the timing is right for him
He will give his time to me?
A double standard stands
Blinded,
Selfish eyes.

Why did I represent myself
Through series of senseless lies?
To protect his image of me?
To give him a sense of pride?
Sit-coms are no longer funny
When his ideals do not come from inside.

21
LITTLE THINGS

Surrounded by thinkers
Pulsing with knowledge
I hide.
Their lips are flickering
Their eyes – Challenging
Their fingers pointing
"Don't you understand?"
I silently nod.
I watch them smirk
I watch them laugh
Over terminology I cannot understand.
Is it truly that difficult?
Vocabulary
This is the key
If I were a thesaurus
I would understand
Their fearful knowledge
Nothing grand.

It is just about the little things
Over looked at hand.
Why not speak little?
-To educate my mind?
Teach me the words
Then they would find
I could converse
or rather enjoy
Their knowledge
as simple
as it is.

22

Position?
Out of proportion?
Out of condition?
Who knows the excess
of light's constant glow.
Its treasure for no one
On earth to behold.
Silence.

Above secret stars
And holes
Lay a dream lover's
Connection and soul.
To find it
Dream
Yet it is not what is seems
For time
and light
alone
Eject the power of what is not known
quite yet.

Forget me not
Forget me yes
Throw all your trust
into that net
of tangles lies
and tangled lines
Walking on the edge
of a fun fulfilled sky.

Please hold the heart
Of broken trust
Do not let go
It needs support
It needs your life
Your love,
Your joy
Do not fondle it
Like a sex toy.

Please understand
What is meant
Is not seen.
For nothing can relate
To a child
In a dream.

23

She always wrote on the paper backwards
Confusion
Excitement
Baffled into one.

She couldn't spell a word
Trifled
Loathsome
Personality become.

She would fly through degraded numbers
Strength
Courage
Rising like the sun.

Good night.

Thunder, Lightening
Pouring down rain
Playing
Carelessly
Psychedelically insane.

Wait.

The land of dreams
Of Peace
Of shame
Drove the spirit
Into her again.

Entranced.

Reality shone into the breeze
Stuffy noses
Wiped on dirty sleeves.
Time begins anew
She fondled with eyes
Deep
Sky blue.

Alone.

The mirror laughed
at her ratted hair.
Her smile
Fake
Her head
in the air.

BANG!

Sleeping beauty
Awakened by dawn
The kiss of faith.
Trust;
Feelings Unknown.
Into hired promises
Demanding
Love.

24

I am shying away at my passion of craft.
My words speak only the colour black.
Who wants to read my self-caused doom.
If spoken in speech, you would leave the room.
Yet everyone wants to figure out lines
In between one's knowledge, one's mind.

Idles like mine (Edgar Allan Poe)
Are mimicked throughout
The words that flow.
Like immortality,
In some sort of way.
Yet who can really understand
The line between night and day?

Good night, Farewell, Sleep tight
In hell.
Please fight your nightmares of defeat
And realize your words you must always keep.
For emotions can hide in tired eyes
And emotional words can tell no lies.

As you wake, tuck tightly
Your pages of words
To read in a new day
When the emotions are not strong
For it will not be long
Until the sun shines bright rays.

Waiting, is the hardest part of all
You may rise
You may fall
But let yourself free from misery
And love yourself
No matter what you see

For no one is more important
No one else can tell
How you truly feel
About living in hell.

25

Do not push the limits of ecstasy
A poisonous stimulant
Beyond the domain of trust.
Love
May truly be
Under curtains of fear.

Please respect unloved ground
It has seen disadvantage
feeling wrong
Under overpowering strengths
Harmful to weak minds.

Believing in love
Body, mind and soul
helps disintegrate
fears from the past.
Psychology cannot explain
Anything belonging
To human thought
Delicate
Is the mind
Hurting to be taught.

Freedom in dreams
Dreams becoming real
Lost in a world
Unprotected
Yet defined.
Release.

26

NAMELESS LOVE

There is but one name you hold
It is not backwards, circular, or upside down
The understanding of this concept
Is hidden in my dreams
Nothing can be counted upon
To be what it seems.

Looking in your eyes has been undirected
Becoming trapped in a wild lovers net.
Precautions are taken under certain situations
When one holds another's heart.

The wonder corrodes my inner soul
Thoughts of dreams coming real
The structure forbids my desire
Questions of how you truly feel.

Time is unanswered and never could be
Pain holds my placid glare
Knowing only what the blue eyes see
Encouraging feelings to be shared.

27

I call out in doubt
to your company
You hear and fly home
With a sweet smile for me.

Your eyes I cannot miss
They are in my dark mind,
Moonlight of the sea
Shining with life.

A MEETING FOR LIFE

Spare some change for your shining eyes
Watch me humiliate my childhood pride
Smile and leave until timeless dreams,
Develop the trust you strive to see.

Nothing new two days later,
Until those eyes return in favour
Showing me of my moments lost
Laughter towards our dual thought.

A spark of light shone through my heart
Joining two shattered, broken parts.
A key formed owning two oak doors,
Healing sharp non-contestant sores.

Toward unknown bounding stars
Finding an eternal filling jar.
New skies above our caressed heads
Co-operatively we wind our separate threads.

Cupids arrow has stabbed through our humble paths
Showing our hearts how love can last.
Feelings shine through our mortal souls
Together, forever becoming whole.

29

The power is a gift
Of harmony and joy.
I can be abused
Like a greedy child's toy.

The love and peace will repel
Your devious adoptions
Entering a dangerous plane
Your mind obsessed with contemption.

Your need ends as the fire burns
And lost in a hole
Covered by the darkest mass
The absence of your soul.

30

Dislike, Anger, Frustration
Seeps out of the hole
Dark thoughts and sensation
Stretches the soul.

Time goes so slowly
During times like this
Deep into eternity it will know
And banish with this kiss.

Bonding quickly, fast for now
Soon it will end again
Take one last huge bow
And in ending time will regain.

Lifeless, Scared, Bare
Maggots creeping in and out
Appearance has no care
The lights have gone out.

31

WASTE

Dry is the rose
Life drained
With a single tear
The fear knows
Only remained
Seen so dear.

Weak defeat
Bowing down
Appearance old
Its waste complete
Left in frown
In the world, sold.

Broken touch
Was once proud
Fuck the world
Pain, too much
Crying aloud
Fallen and curled.

32

Threatened in surrounding time
Crushed by fated lies
Everything leads to crime
Behind those cloudy blue eyes.

Childhood nightmares are true
Facing the painful days
Drawn down and faced blue
The world against you plays.

Insanity only you know
Owning only personal hate
Why is this so?
Falling down, crumbling
Unable to wait.

Eternal soul eaten away
Mind lost in tears
Who cares what they say
Live through your disastrous fears.

33

BOREDOM

The song is so lovely
About the world
And its fakeness;
Nothing is real.
It is so lonely
Alone,
In a ball curled
Drawing in sadness
Someone can feel.

Pain so deep
Hiding your feelings
Nervous of what to think.
Wondering who you are
Talking a peep
At the endless ceiling
Spotting the kink
Not able to see too far.

Why are you here?
Asking yourself
What purpose is living?
It is all a game.
The truth is near,
The picture on the shelf
You are now crying
Everything is the same.

34

THE ONE EARED RABBIT

The one eared rabbit stands
On his own, curled in sadness.
No one would give him a hand
In his tired mess.

He tries to walk on
Corrupted by falling walls
Captured by life's con
Picking himself up after he falls.

Destruction begins again
During times with unabled thoughts
Through misery remains
Nothing left of what he was taught.

Everlasting mistakes
Drag the poor freak down
Love, hope and happiness are fake
All he can do is frown.

GRAVE

The tombs of thought
Guard my deceased dreams
Cold; stiff soil
Hide my treasured being.

While up above shines
The full spherical moon
Masking the far dark sky.

And beyond our sun
Is unknown, remaining
An unsatisfying human grace.

To know, to believe, to hope
People suffer in failure
Not able to stand against
The treasury of limitations.

The mind, a character in its own,
Differs from the norm,
The soulless, demanding norm;
My sun doesn't shine.

The eclipse controls the frequencies of hope.
The dream of living
The knowledge of why we must shine.
My tiered faults drive away my pride.
Left alone,
To be alone,
the comfort, the silence
In my selfish dead world.

36

LOVE'S INNOCENCE

He watches,
calmly
Above the city lights
Hidden between two gargoyles
Distant nocturnal sight.

Appearing below,
A tired mess
Curled beneath a box
Quietly at rest.

He focuses sharply
No witness to stir
His blood thirst quenching
—intentful murderer.

Soaring down
to level ground
He stalks his victim.

So soft,
So silent,
His dreams in formation.

Her beauty shone through
The mask of dirt upon her face.
How could such beauty
Belong to the human race?

He stepped toward her gently
Caressing her presence's air
No blood could be drawn
From such an innocent glare!

Lifting her from her cardboard doom
She startles in screams
Testing his gloom.

Softly trancing
The young woman in
His cold, dead arms
He begins to fly
Away from dawns' noisy cars.

She awoke from a challenging dream
Only to find a mystery.
Confused about her location
She walked around
Noticing she was naked.

Down a long corridor
She tiptoed lightly
Looking for clothes
To secure her tightly.

Turning right, a portrait infeared her glare
The man in her nightmare,
He was right there!
—or a relative upon the wall,
It was dated before the first brawl.

She continued on her way
Finding a curtain upon a duvet.

Gently she wound the velvet around
Her cold, tired body.
Then came a sound.
She sharply turned her frightful head,
It was the man,
From her dream,
From the portrait.
"Shouldn't you be dead?"

His toothy grin
Revealed sharp fangs
"Don't worry my beauty
Mythology is sane."

Shocked at the charming, romantic sight
She clenched her fists in utter fright.
"But no, you couldn't be
—What the hell do you want from me?"

He looked deep within her eyes
"Nothing.
Your innocence must survive."
He approached her in her conscious state.
She trembled softly but could not wait.
His touch so gentle,
Could only sooth
Her forgotten path
Her hazardous moods.

Melting in his ecstasy
She stared into his eyes
So bravely.
He spoke, "My child,
Will you be a part of me,
Preserve your beauty for eternity?"

She questioned the thought
Then panicked inside
"But will I lose my soul?"

He lowered his guard
Shedding a tear
"I'm so sorry,
My greed overcame what's dear.
Young love,
Young beauty,
You must leave.
My instincts rise above
What my heart may perceive.
I do not want to harm
Such innocence
Such grace.
Please leave now
I can no longer bare seeing
Your tempting face."

Confused by the supposive blood thirsty beast
She looked outside,
Gazed in inner peace and said,
"This world is not meant for me,
Nor you.
Let me stay
What you need is what you'll do.
You're the only one who knows I exist.
Please let me tempt you,
Do not be hesitant.
I do need my soul
And my innocence alone
But with you I'll own a different throne."

He looked at her with hopeful gloom,
"Alas,
Not now.
You are still a child.
Experience this world
So when you die
You can choose your freedom
And fly
To a paradise beyond our sky."

He returned her back upon the street
Marking the last time their saddened eyes meet.

37

PEOPLE

People are people
Filled with disguises, surprises, devices
To win your trusting eyes.
A phoney smile, an inner laugh,
Who can decide which ones are lies?

Dedication, determination, devastation
Push their bodies far
Into actions, reactions
And painful stresses
When they are pushed too far.

Spending life following faded dreams
People blindly, accept their deeds
Knowing nothing is all it means
And oddly, not what it seems.

Living birth until Death
Farcing their deities
Structured penalties, chastity, and societies
Give them mortal hope.
Emotionless boxes filled with light
Prevent people from moping.

Universal confusion, insecure stable minds.
Galactic thoughts stab through earth's time.

Always dreaming for something else
Curses the people's paths
Subconscious rules
Logic lost.
Some people let go of themselves.

Most however play the game,
Cultural horizons unite
Slowly as madnesses engage
Peace, love, light.

Too bad there is so much pain.

If people could accept changing
Colours, weathers, and clothes
Something extraordinary will remain
Undetectable by prose.

Surprise the atmosphere
Underlying the stars
Violence greed and hunger
Have horridly stretched too far.

If people could see people
In everyone they meet
It could fill Pandora's box
And with it
Pain's defeat.

BEGINNING

It seems so long
My sliver in time
Yet a new spark
In the sun will shine.
Broken hearts,
Broken mind
Will repair along the turning vine
Coiled and thorned
But not so fast
For time will not forever last.
Dreams forbid my reality,
Slipping away
In my lost identity.
Who will I be when I again begin
Ignoring years of faithless sin?
Always aborting structure's lies
Will I give in to those firm eyes
Who watch my every distasteful mood
Yet it is not I who choose to brood
On images, farcing normalities way
Of living a plain world day by day.

Success was never a question before
In this new world a term to explore
Above the ground
I will not fly
But soar
Opening those once locked, hardwood doors.
Behind which I cannot see
But filled with a sense
What is, is what will be.

39

PROBLEM

Fine words spoken
Problem
A problem is trying to rise
A problem is your dull eyes
When timing is only right
To erase my fantasies
Not enough dependability
Has led into lies.
When truths are broadly spoken
You reverse them
Into your make-believe
Of make-believing me.

She faced more horror
Morbid anger, pain
Yet she can see past
(what faults you last)
And see
I'm not insane.

Your world and mine
Parallel
Forget your pride
Farewell

Never will my dreams
Be torn apart
By your "Ever-caring"
fathered heart.

40
DAY TIME DRAMA

Arriving from a month of hibernation
Friendly glances, flashing smiles,
Insane formulations,
Awakened my hope of self-contained freedom.

Noticing creatures never seen before
Walking down the street
Reflecting sunlight's bore.
Wall rats, hidden from society's eyes
Awaken from somewhere devoured in lies.

Encouragement developed along their paths
Their aching addictions, beliefs,
Can no longer last.
For the dawn's glorious dew
Absorbed into
Their dry night's swollen sores.

The rest of the world looks at the creatures with dismay
Yet broad enough, the future
Will see them every day.

One world,
Broken
Into trillions of parts
May finally unite
With a compassionate heart.

Acceptance of the old, young
Ragged and clothed
Appears beyond the sun set's
Miles of gold.

We have been shocked so much
Differences finally agree
That everyone is equal
As long as in the eyes
A soul is seen.

41

HOSTAGE CRISIS

Five hostages sit in a room
Staring at terror's eyes
Awaiting their impending doom
Haunted by fate's cries.

ONE held proud shows nothing of fear.
Laughing at the man of glass
Shedding a single tear
Washing away his mask.

TWO shivers curled in a tight ball.
Hiding from the shattered man
Screams out, "Catch me before I fall"
Admitting years of sin.

THREE lay still against the cold floor.
Silencing a cold sound
Of opening and closing doors
Behind, his wife is bound.

FOUR recites his prophecy
To the terrorist trend,
"You're going to die before I flee,
To hell your soul I'll send!"

FIVE laughs at the others detail
Pulling out a shiny blade
And hurls it through the stuffy air.
FOUR's prophecy is made.

A man tears in the once locked door
Thinking the scream was fun
Then seeing his friend on the floor.
And FIVE with his friend's gun.

Dropping down on his shaking knees
He looks at FIVE's stern eyes
"I am so sorry, don't kill me please."
One shot, and the man dies.

The five swallow their present fears
Unloading the fierce gun
THREE runs to his sore wife in tears
The end has just begun.

42

FOR WHOM THE WORDS SPEAK

For whom the bell tolls
Was a sacred ballad
For rage-stricken children
Whose souls were not valid.

For whom the sky cries
Was a fable of tears
Drenching the tired children
Washing away their fears.

For whom the sun shines
Was an energy of brilliance
Yet the children burned
As their minds caught diligence.

For whom the fear reigns
Was left alone, trapped in sadness
Smothered the tiny children
Destined to thoughts of madness.

For whom death strikes
Was peace, fate, and sleep
The children began to worship
A god for their souls to keep.

For whom existence believes
Was the ideal mankind
The amount of devastated children
To disease the human mind.

43

Foolish means
on foolish days
Creates a place
for the mind to play.

Interfering with trust
Respect
and Love
                        Lost
in a world
Where consciousness is a must.

Shitty, pity
shitty deal
How does the junkie
Truly feel?

No mind
No how
No where
Is the junkie truly there?

Ask the fool
who knows all
Claiming charm and aspect
Preventing the fall.

Damn confusion
Damn lies
Give a chance to innocent eyes.

Hold tightly the aching heart
Pulsing
To help you motivate the start
For security
For dreams
For an understanding
of what it all means.

Confusion reigns
as the pouring rain
falls beneath earth's core.
Drenched people burn
and choose to turn
Chancing the
Smothering
Stabbing sores.

The hour is up
disappointment
Greed.
Where is the soil
to plant the seed?

Distant decisions
Harm the heart
Claim prosperity
Although so apart.

Need
Plays a major role
If apart from love
Apart from the soul.
So stay
Where you belong.
For how can that feeling
Be the least bit wrong?

Watch loosely the fool
Playing only his rule
Intelligent bases
His smiling faces
Staying cool
Calm
Dancing freely
to a free song.

If the fool's eyes
Change bright
To dull
Hold him tightly
Hold him close
And full.

For love like this
Helps junkies strive
Other things important
For their lives.
(Away from their disease).

The entertainment may die
When tears in the eye
But Again
Watch the fool
For he knows
How you truly feel
And he cares
He does
Although he may be a fool
He knows a lot
About natural rule
And he will help you see
That love
Is all you need
To Be!

MAGIC LOVE

Throughout the threads of timeless agony
A star shone light rays carrying
A heart filled song.

The misty past led unbelievable lust
Teasing the heart's mind.
Finding solemn joy, everlasting trust,
Between two lost souls.

Lightening stabs through the cold hateful plain.
Love seeps through the tierless dropping rain.

Connecting astronomical powers unknown,
You are my Lord,
I am your Crone.

45

A FRIENDS LOST IDENTITY

Her salty tears stung my churning heart.
She rose, ran, and smashed against the wall.
I see her. I run to catch her fall.
Katherine, sweet Katherine
Don't let go.

My words switch her bodily control.
"Cheryl, I love you, but no one cares!"
Her pain, smashing pain…..
STOP HER FROM CRUSHING HER SKULL!
She rose in laughter;
Madness.

Reality Katherine, you are still here
Quit shocking my soul with your rage.
Give up, let the pain go.
Please, I am here
Can't you hear me call?
Her head flinched from side to side
Sounds of trapped animals release from her mind.
Silence.

I glare down at my beloved friend
Quivering from neglected faults
All I want to do is help.
She cries and flashes her scornful eyes
"Stop the evil Cheryl, It's here!
STOP IT!"
Desperately I scope the room,
Nothing but walls,
Nothing but doom.

Dear Katherine, I sadly realize,
It is your battle
It is up to you to decide.
Quit wasting your life
Filling it with lies
You are valuable,
You are beautiful,
Can't you see past that shattered wall?
I can't be there, every time you fall.

46

FAILURE

No more family doctors, dentists, or pride
Hiding away
the feelings inside.
Walking through door
to door.
Presenting identity
New prescriptions to explore.

Health, disease, illness, "Oh please!
Let me be healthy once more."
Without the love
From creator
to child
Health walks out the door.

Mental healing,
Tearful thoughts
Confused learnings,
Nothing new taught.
Yet personal understanding
Wherever to start
Knowing within this life
It is a huge part.

Scattered income.
Scattered thoughts,
Organization
Has yet to be taught.

Being bought out
Through troubled times
Only gave false freedoms
independency
gave lies.

Experience always needed
to become taxed fines
Education depleted
available time.
A true thought forming rhyme
enters the new year
to add knowledge to the time.
But now, swatting flies
Why did this happen
Just before the time to rise?

Now
He apologises.
(He is moving in two weeks)
"Oh, sorry girl,
You're not stupid,
You are sweet."

A disrespectful hallowing
on the full moon.
His doubled standard accusations
hallow in the mood.

How could a father
insist a child's doom
How could a father
destroy a child's tune.

Faithlessly walking
in alleys
on streets
taking off the shoes
airing calloused feet.

Tears.
Hopelessness.
Fear.

Memories haunt present gifts
for father thinks he has made up for all of this.

Well, he hasn't.

Tried to reconcile.
Tried to make his love worthwhile.
Tried to forgive.
Tried to forget.
FAILED.

47

A tiny mouse crawls out of its hole
Sniffing opportunities fresh air.
It scurries across the wide kitchen floor
Looking at new terrain to explore.

High above, the light shone dim
Making visibility scarce
Yet the mouse ventures on
Despite uncertain sights
Allowing itself to decide
On an uncertain whim.

Days pass slowly
The mouse scurries round
The first floor of the house,
Unacknowledging its hole.

It nibbles on crumbs and bits of cheese
Provided by the housewife's
Occupation's necessities.

Still questioning its twisted path
The mouse tries to lie down and relax.
A big black cat walks through the front door,
Had spent months on the street feeding,
And looking for more.

The mouse tenses,
The cat pounces,
Running round and round,
The mouse runs into its hole
It had previously found.

Knowing that the hole
Was no place to survive
It ponders a plan
To allow its freedom outside.

The cat lies asleep
Beside the mouse's hole
Dreaming of the mouse
On a cinnamon roll.

The mouse gears up
In disguise for its plan
Placing on tiny cat ears
And covering itself in sand.

It slowly marches past the sleeping cat
Walking softly on four feet
Climbs up on to a padded chair
And pretends to sleep.

The cat wakes and stretches,
Pawing inside the hole.
His claw catches something interesting
And drags it out.
It was a note.

"Dear Mister Cat," the note did read
"I've left your humble home,
And have taken everything I need."

The cat looked around questionably
To see where the mouse could be.
Then he saw something odd,
On his chair sound asleep.

The cat walked over proudly
And rudely pawed the thing.
The mouse awoke startled,
(It almost began to scream).

"Who and what are you?"
Asked the boggled cat.
"I'm a tiny kitten,
My name is Nat."
(The mouse was quite afraid
But continued with his act).

"Why are you here?"
The cat questioned again,
Sniffing the apparent kitten
Staring at it in vain.

"Well, the housewife just had a baby,
So she brought me home for her new child.
A newborn person a newborn cat,
What could be more wild?"

"Your youth displeases me."
The cat cried unhappily.
"Since the mouse is gone
And a new cat is here,
There is no room for me.
I shall leave this humble home
And find more mice for hunting."

The cat in despair
Walked away from the chair
And out the front door.

The mouse shook off the sand
And jumped with glee
For now the entire house
Was his to be.

AFTERWORD

When I was younger, I made up my own words when I wrote. There are a few words included in the poems that are not official words. However, I left these in. Poetry is an avenue for creating and bringing deep thoughts and feelings alive. An entity is created within each poem carrying a message, emotion, creativity, and thought. After reviewing some of my writing in university, an English teacher said to me, "You break all the rules before knowing them." She went on to say that this is not a bad thing, however if you learn the rules you will have so much more to work with.

Poetry is a place to break the rules of writing. It is also a place where if you know the rules you can create beautiful works of art. Similarly, in life you can choose to create your own rules, break existing social rules, or follow social rules. Your life is your creation. How you live and what you follow is a choice. Living on the street is breaking a social rule of choosing comfort, and at the same time some people are actually more comfortable living on the street. We are born into a world that tells us what is comfortable, what is normal, and what is expected. We can create in those confines, or we can create our own confines. Poetry is a beautiful avenue to safely explore breaking or following rules. On the following pages are the definitions of my made up words.

DEFINITIONS

Contemption: Full of contempt. It is also like taking action out of contempt, or a feeling of contempt. (Page 69)

Devastational: Full of devastation. (Page 27)

Fakeness: Something that has the quality of being fake. (Page 77)

Infeared: In fear, causing fear and also partially in reference to the word infrared (ie: seeing truth, sensing and detecting something to be fearful of); an accurate supposition of something to be fearful of. (Page 85)

Intentful: To be full of intent. Intending fully. (Page 83)

Jonesed: A word used for when someone is needing drugs, "jonesing" for drugs. (I did not create this word, it is widely used among drug users but is still not included in contemporary dictionaries). (Page 45)

Madnesses: A group of madness, or groups of madness. (Page 90)

Remoteless: Having no control, not coming from a source, not being controlled (a "remote", as in how remote controls control things). Also, remote as in a place far away (remoteless is not far away either, it is close). (Page 43)

Supposive: Supposed. (Page 87)

Thorned: Covered in thorns. (Page 93)

Tierless: From the word tiered, (layered). Tierless means not layered. In the poem example the rain is all coming down at once all in the same direction, "Love seeps through the tierless dropping rain". (Page 107)

Unabled: Not able to, something is preventing you from doing something, or feeling something. (Page 79)

Note on abstract words having ownership by using "'s".
Within these poems I give abstract words ownership of something by using an 's such as: normality's lies, transportation's seed, equality's bounds , structure's lies, and occupation's necessities. These words are social constructs and social constructs do in some regard own us, especially when we believe in their importance.

Art by Cheryl Fountain

ABOUT THE AUTHOR

Cheryl Fountain spent the later part of her teen life living on the streets of Toronto. As an adult she became an author, property manager, editor, Emotional Wisdom Trainer, and earned a Bachelor Degree in Social Work from the University of Regina in Canada. She utilizes her skills and experience to support others in their journeys discovering their own unique potentials, and bringing more of their inner selves out and into the world. Cheryl grew up in Ontario Canada, and spent 17 years living in the Canadian Arctic. She followed her dream moving closer to the Rocky Mountains, and now calls Alberta her home.

Follow Cheryl on Facebook or contact her at her webpage:

www.facebook.com/CherylFountainAuthor
www.cherylfountain.com

Other works by Cheryl:
- Assertiveness: A Life Changing Communication Skill
- I Love My Family

Coming Soon
- Sock Soup- Spring 2022
- The Little Goose That Could- Fall 2022

Thank you for reading! Please add a short review on Amazon and let me know what you thought!

Manufactured by Amazon.ca
Bolton, ON